EAT YOUR WAY TO

Success

FAME AND

Fortune

**LAGOON
BOOKS**

Project Editor: Sylvia Goulding
Book Design: Norma Martin

Thanks to Mike Goulding, Lesley Robb, Simon Farnhell, Ray Leaning and Sarah Carne, Nick Daws
and Ann Marangos

Cover Design: River Design. www.riverdesign.com

Series Editor: Lucy Dear
Visual concept: Sarah Wells
Based on original concept by Simon Melhuish

Published by:
LAGOON BOOKS
PO BOX 311, KT2 5QW, UK
PO BOX 990676, Boston, MA 02199, USA
www.lagoongames.com

ISBN: 1902813618

© LAGOON Books, 2001

Printed in Hong Kong.

Introduction

Gunning for success? On the fast track to fame and fortune? There's no point beating around the bush—you need this book.

Here are the facts. If you're going to be a success at anything, from showbiz to commerce, you can't afford to be half-hearted about it. And that applies to food just like anything else. Cook like a pauper and that's how you'll stay. Cook like a million dollars and that's what you'll end up worth. Can't believe it? You'd better. Here's a taste of what's to come in this gilt-edged guide to culinary achievement...

BODY AND SOUL

The longest journey begins with a single step, and in Chapter 1 we feature light, healthy foods which will set you on the path to success. From *Star-Struck Chicken Salad* to *Brain-Booster Swordfish and Bean Salsa*, these tasty dishes will feed your mind as well as your body. They'll give you that vital edge, ensuring you're all ready to grasp that golden opportunity when it comes knocking.

KNOCK 'EM OUT

True success requires has to be recognized—and this high-powered chapter will push you into the limelight. Blockbusting recipes, from *Show-Stealing Salmon Baguettes* to *Flamin' Fillets of Pork*, will show your dinner guests you mean business. Offers of contracts and highly paid jobs should follow swiftly after.

IMMORTAL SOULS

Most successful people have role-models. So in Chapter 3 you'll find a selection of classic recipes inspired by great figures from the past. From *Best Beef Wellington* to *Chicken Tetrazzini Treat*, these delicious dishes have stood the test of time. Cook them, serve them, eat them, and let their creators' fame inspire you to still greater results.

SWEET SUCCESS

Hard work is the recipe for your success, of course—but sometimes sweet-talking is the only way to ensure that your achievements are fairly rewarded. And so our final chapter features ten utterly delicious desserts, from *Lord of the Castle* to *Prize-Winning Pear Tart*, to sweeten up your guests and boost your bid for fame and fortune.

This book may be small, but don't be deceived —it's dynamite. They say every top man or woman has their own recipe for success—well, here you have over forty. Remember: when the going gets tough, the tough get cooking. So what are you waiting for? Turn the page and start making these seriously successful dishes! Fame and fortune beckon!

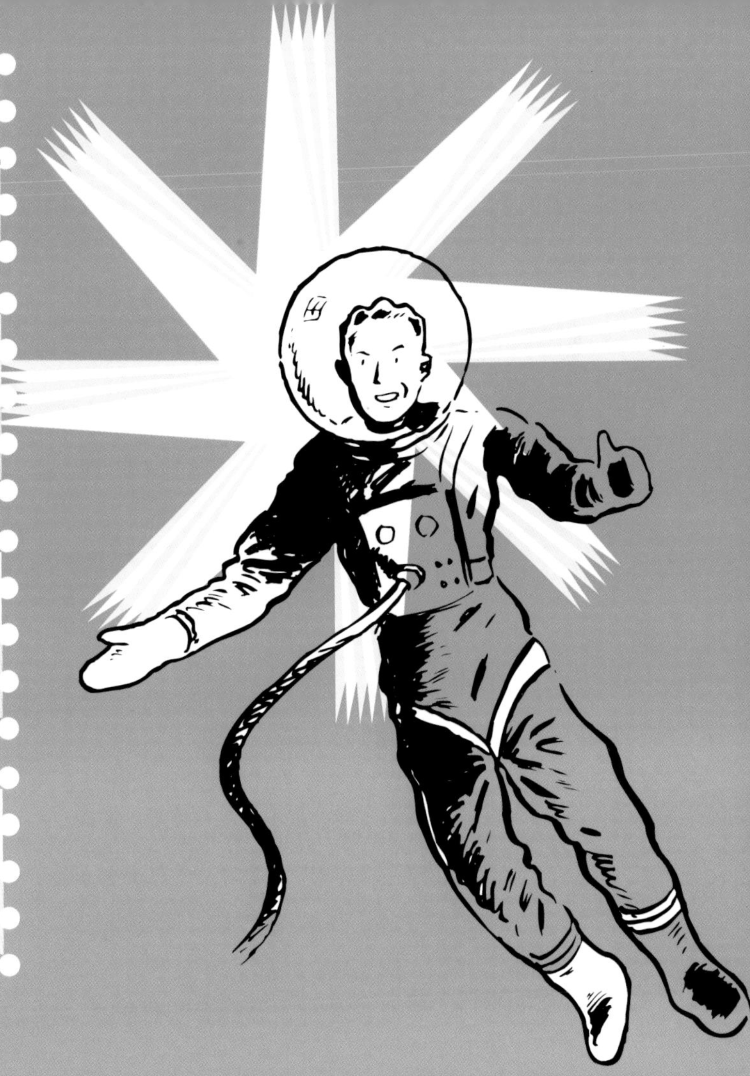

CHAPTER 1

Body and Soul

FEEL-GOOD FOOD TO PUT
YOU ONE STEP AHEAD

EAT THE RIGHT FOOD WHEN EVERY SECOND COUNTS AND YOU NEED TO BE ON FULL ALERT...

Contents

Shooting-Star Salad

You too can be a movie star in your own kitchen! One bite of this slim-sational salad and you'll feel yourself transported to the red carpets of Hollywood!

SERVES 2

+ 1 tsp clear honey
+ 1 tsp hot mustard

WHAT TO BUY

+ 2 handfuls of mixed salad leaves (eg rocket and lamb's lettuce)
+ 125 g/4 ½ oz cooked large prawns (shrimps)
+ 1 red (bell) pepper, cut into strips
+ 1 green (bell) pepper, cut into strips
+ 1 ripe avocado, sliced
+ 2 star fruit, sliced horizontally

Star-struck dressing:
+ Juice of ½ fresh lime
+ 1 tbsp olive oil

HOW TO COOK IT

1 Wash the salad leaves and roughly tear them, then divide them evenly between two plates. Arrange the other ingredients as follows: place the avocado slices in a fan shape around the plate, then arrange the prawns (shrimps) and (bell) peppers in between, and distribute the heavenly star fruit on top.

2 In a small jar, blend all the dressing ingredients together and season to taste with salt and pepper. Drizzle the dressing over the top of the salad.

3 Enjoy this star-shaped wonder and you'll soon be rising like a comet yourself!

Seriously Rich Chive Soup

Rich beyond your wildest dreams—and yet this gorgeous soup made from humble garden chives will still leave you with room for more!

SERVES 4

WHAT TO BUY

+ 450 g/l lb floury potatoes
+ 25 g/l oz butter
+ I bay leaf
+ I liter/35 fl oz fresh chicken stock
+ 100 ml/3 fl oz dry white wine or sherry
+ Salt and pepper
+ 450 ml/15 fl oz milk
+ 100 g/4 oz fresh chives
+ Single (light) cream to serve

HOW TO COOK IT

1 Peel the potatoes, and slice them about finger-thick. Melt the butter in a large saucepan. Add the potato slices and the bay leaf to the pan and cook for about 2 minutes, stirring occasionally.

2 Add the stock, wine or sherry, and season to taste. Bring to the boil, then reduce the heat, cover with a lid and simmer gently for about 15 minutes, or until the potatoes are soft.

3 Add the milk and heat through without boiling again. Remove the bay leaf.

4 Reserve a few blades of chives. Put the remaining chives into the blender together with a few spoonfuls of the soup base and blend until completely smooth.

5 Add the puréed chives to the soup, stir well to combine and heat through for 1–2 minutes.

6 To serve, snip the remaining chives. Garnish the soup with a good sprinkling of chives and a generous swirl of cream—your guests will never guess this soup was growing in your own backyard!

BETWEEN SOUP AND LOVE, SOUP IS BETTER... (OLD SPANISH SAYING)

Let's Eat

CHIVES, IF EATEN REGULARLY, WILL STIMULATE THE APPETITE. SO, IF YOU OFTEN GET TAKEN OUT FOR BUSINESS LUNCHES, THIS CHIVE SOUP IS THE PERFECT STARTER—IT WILL ENSURE THAT YOU CAN GET THROUGH THE MAIN COURSE AND THE DESSERT WITHOUT UPSETTING YOUR BUSINESS PARTNERS!

Supreme Spinach 'n' Cheese Rolls

Packed with iron for stamina, these delicious rolls will keep you going through the longest board meeting–and ensure you're still wide-awake enough to clinch that vital deal...

SERVES 4

WHAT TO BUY

+ 450 g/l lb baby spinach leaves
+ Salt and pepper
+ 2 sheets filo pastry
+ 25 g/l oz butter
+ 100 g/4 oz Greek goats' cheese

HOW TO COOK IT

1 Heat the oven to 200°C/400°F/Gas Mark 6.

2 Wash and shred the spinach leaves. Do not shake dry, but place them into a large saucepan over a low heat. Cook for about 3 minutes, stirring occasionally, or until the spinach has wilted a little. Season to taste and allow to cool.

3 Roll out the filo pastry and quickly brush the sheets with generous amounts of melted butter. (Do not leave the pastry lying about without the butter–it will quickly dry out.) Reserve some of the butter. Place the pastry sheets on top of each other and cut into 4 squares.

4 Divide the wilted spinach equally between the pastry squares. Crumble the goats' cheese over the spinach, then roll up the squares to make individual rolls. Tuck in the ends as you are rolling them up, so that the spinach and cheese filling will not ooze out.

5 Place the rolls on a baking sheet and brush with the remaining butter. Place in the oven and cook for about 15–20 minutes, or until golden brown.

6 Serve immediately. Accompany with a tomato and basil salad for a light appetizer, or serve 2 rolls per person, with mixed long-grain and wild rice for a main course—you're just so talented!

THE NICE THING ABOUT BEING A CELEBRITY IS THAT WHEN YOU BORE PEOPLE, THEY THINK IT'S THEIR FAULT...
(HENRY KISSINGER)

Food 4 Thought

THE GREEK PHILOSOPHER ARISTOTLE, ONE OF THE GREATEST THINKERS OF ALL TIME, WAS A HUGE FAN OF GREEK CHEESES. NOW, WAS IT HIS LOVE FOR FETA WHICH GAVE HIM HIS GREATEST INSIGHTS? MAKE IT YOUR MOTTO IN LIFE TOO: I EAT, THEREFORE I AM.

Great Gatsby's Grilled Vegetables

The best-dressed vegetables in town— a culinary masterpiece coming soon to a kitchen near you!

SERVES 4

WHAT TO BUY

+ 200 g/7 oz fine green beans
+ 8 rashers (strips) bacon
+ 6 tbsp oilve oil
+ I aubergine (eggplant), trimmed and halved
+ 4 canned artichoke hearts, drained
+ I green (bell) pepper, quartered and seeded
+ I red (bell) pepper, quartered and seeded
+ 200 g/7 oz large mushrooms, cleaned and halved
+ I courgette (zucchini), sliced
+ Juice of 2 lemons
+ 2 tbsp coriander seeds, crushed

For the garlic mayo:

+ 2 egg yolks
+ 6 garlic cloves, crushed
+ 6 tbsp olive oil
+ Salt and pepper

HOW TO COOK IT

1 Make the garlic mayo: put the egg yolks in a bowl, add the garlic, and beat with a hand-held whisk until everything is well combined. Add the oil: first add a few drops and whisk, then add the remainder, whisking all the time, until you have a creamy sauce. Season to taste with salt, pepper, and lemon juice.

2 Heat the barbecue or the grill. Divide the beans into four portions, then wrap 2 rashers (strips) of bacon

16

around each portion to create a little bundle. Slice the aubergine (eggplant) halves.

3 In a small bowl, combine the oil, the lemon juice, and the coriander. Brush all the vegetables with this mixture, then grill for 25–30 minutes, or until they're cooked and nicely charred.

4 Serve the grilled vegetables—and make sure everyone helps themselves to the garlic mayo!

A BIG MAN HAS NO TIME REALLY TO DO ANYTHING BUT JUST SIT AND BE BIG... (F. SCOTT FITZGERALD)

Artichoke Fame

NOT ONLY ARE MEDITERRANEAN VEGETABLES, SUCH AS THESE EXCEPTIONALLY NUTRITIOUS, PUTTING YOU FIRMLY IN THE LEAD, THEY MIGHT ALSO GIVE YOU EXTRA SEX APPEAL. IN 1947, MARYLIN MONROE WAS CROWNED THE FIRST QUEEN OF ARTICHOKES—AND WHO COULD WISH FOR MORE FAME AND SUCCESS?

Lucky Luciano's Favorite Pizza

Make your dinner guests an offer they can't refuse. Serve up this classic of Italian cuisine-pizza just like Mamma used to make!

SERVES 4

WHAT TO BUY

+ 100 g/4 oz plain (all-purpose) flour
+ 60 g/2 ½ oz butter, diced
+ I small egg
+ 4 tomatoes, cut into thick slices
+ 2 tsp olive oil
+ 5-6 mini Mozzarellas, cut into thick slices
+ 4 spring onions (scallions), chopped
+ I tbsp fresh rosemary, chopped
+ Salt and pepper

HOW TO COOK IT

1 In a large bowl, combine the flour and the butter, using a hand-held whisk, until you have a crumbly mixture.

2 In a small bowl beat the egg and about 4 tsp cold water. Gradually add this egg mixture to the flour while continuing to beat. When the mixture starts to form a smooth ball and comes away from the sides of the bowl, turn it out onto a floured surface. Knead with lightly floured hands to form a soft dough. Cover in clingfilm (plastic wrap) and chill for 30 minutes.

3 Heat the oven to 200°C/400°F/Gas Mark 6. Roll out the pastry and shape to fit a 23 cm/9 in loose-bottomed cake tin. Put the pastry into the tin and trim the edges. Cover with a sheet of baking paper cut to size, and cover this with a layer of baking beans or rice.

4 Bake for 15 minutes, then remove the beans or rice and paper and bake for another 10 minutes, or until the pastry is a golden color. Cool and reduce the oven to 170°C/325°F/Gas Mark 3.

5 Place the tomatoes in a separate baking dish, drizzle with oil and bake for 30 minutes to caramelize. Increase the oven to 180°C/350°F/Gas Mark 4.

6 Arrange the tomato and Mozzarella slices alternately on the pizza base, and sprinkle with the spring onions (scallions) and rosemary. Season, bake for 10 minutes.

7 Serve with a glass of blood-red Italian Valpolicella—and keep your eyes on the door.

Think Positive

AN ACCIDENT, OFTEN THE MOTHER OF INVENTION, IS SAID TO HAVE LED TO THE FIRST PRODUCTION OF MOZZARELLA CHEESE: IN A CHEESE FACTORY NEAR NAPLES, CHEESE CURDS ACCIDENTALLY FELL INTO HOT WATER. THE MORAL OF THIS TALE: EVERY MISTAKE IS ALSO AN OPPORTUNITY WAITING TO BE GRASPED!

SUCCESS IS THAT OLD ABC — ABILITY, BREAKS, AND COURAGE...
(CHARLES LUCKMAN)

19

Star-Struck Chicken Salad

Lights! Camera! Action! Then cue this blockbusting main course salad and stand by for the rave reviews!

SERVES 4

WHAT TO BUY

+ 2 tbsp vegetable oil
+ 4 chicken breasts
+ 1 cm/½ in cube fresh ginger, finely chopped
+ 3 star anise, crushed
+ 3 tbsp sherry
+ 125 ml/4 fl oz/½ cup chicken stock
+ 3 garlic cloves, crushed
+ 2 bay leaves
+ 175 ml/6 fl oz/¾ cup olive oil
+ 175 ml/6 fl oz/¾ cup white wine vinegar
+ 2 onions, sliced

+ Salt and pepper
+ Baby spinach leaves and lemon wedges to serve

HOW TO COOK IT

1 Heat the oil in a saucepan. Skin the chicken and slice the meat into finger-sized strips. Add the chicken to the pan together with the ginger and star anise, and fry for about 5 minutes, stirring, until lightly browned all over.

2 Pour in the sherry and stock. Reduce the heat and simmer for 20 minutes, stirring occasionally, until the chicken is tender.

3 Lift out the chicken and pat dry with kitchen paper. In a bowl, combine the garlic, bay leaves, olive oil, vinegar, and onions. Stir well, then season to taste with salt and pepper.

4 Add the chicken strips to the bowl and stir to coat evenly. Leave to marinate overnight before serving.
5 Serve the chicken salad on a bed of spinach leaves, and garnish with the lemon wedges. Wait for the compliments to roll in.

I DON'T KNOW MUCH ABOUT BEING A MILLIONAIRE, BUT I'LL BET I'D BE DARLING AT IT...
(DOROTHY PARKER)

Spice Star

STAR ANISE IS THE STAR IN THIS DISH. THE MOST DECORATIVE OF ALL SPICES, IT ALSO IMPARTS A POWERFUL ANISEED FLAVOR—EXCELLENT FOR CLEANSING THE PALATE BEFORE AN IMPORTANT SPEECH. AND YOU COULD ALWAYS ADD EXTRA FRESHNESS WITH A GLASS OF ANISEED-FLAVORED DRINK SUCH AS PERNOD OR RICARD!

Top Hot Dog

Enjoy top dog status every time with this sizzling supper-time special-proof (if it were needed) that sometimes the simplest ideas really are the best!

SERVES 4

WHAT TO BUY

+ 25 g/1 oz butter
+ 4 good-quality sausages with garlic and herbs
+ 4 onions, sliced
+ 4 juniper berries, crushed
+ A few sprigs of oregano, chopped
+ A small glass of Marsala wine or sherry
+ 4 tsp French mustard
+ Salt and pepper
+ 4 small ciabattas (or 2 large, cut in half)
+ 1 beefsteak tomato, cut into eight slices

HOW TO COOK IT

1 In a large frying pan, melt the butter and then add the sausages. Do not prick the sausage skin. Cook over a gentle heat for about 15 minutes, turning occasionally, until browned all over.

2 Remove the sausages from the pan and keep them warm. Add the onion slices and cook for about 5 minutes, stirring occasionally to loosen the sausage fat in the pan, until they are nicely colored.

3 Add the juniper berries and the oregano, and continue cooking for 2 minutes, stirring to prevent the onions from burning.

4 Add the Marsala or sherry and the mustard, and season to taste. Stir, and turn the heat up to high to reduce the liquid a bit. Cook for another 2-3 minutes, stirring occasionally, then return the sausages to the pan to warm them through.

5 Assemble the hot dogs: cut the ciabattas open lengthways. Halve the sausages lengthways and place two halves on each ciabatta bottom. Spoon the onions from the pan over the sausages, then pour over some of the gravy. Top with two tomato slices and cover with the top half of the ciabatta.

6 Serve with a first-class beer, turn on the TV to watch the World Cup, and prepare to rule the world.

> TELL ME WHAT
> YOU EAT AND
> I WILL TELL YOU
> WHAT YOU ARE...
> (A. BRILLAT-SAVARIN)

Doodle Fame

NEWSPAPER CARTOONIST TAD DORGAN, UNDER PRESSURE AND SHORT OF IDEAS, NOTICED A SAUSAGE VENDOR AND QUICKLY SKETCHED A CARTOON OF A DACHSHUND IN A ROLL. HIS SPELLING WAS NOT TOO HOT, SO INSTEAD OF 'DACHSHUND', HE JUST SCRAWLED 'HOT DOG' ON TOP, AND THE NAME CAUGHT ON. SO, DON'T BIN YOUR PHONE-SIDE DOODLES, CHECK IF YOU CAN COIN A PHRASE FIRST!

THE ONLY PLACE WHERE SUCCESS COMES BEFORE WORK IS IN THE DICTIONARY...
(VIDAL SASSOON)

Dog Eat Dog

CRABS ARE PARTIAL TO THE ODD OYSTER—IN FACT, THEY HAVE BEEN KNOWN CLEAN OUT ENTIRE OYSTER BEDS! SO, BY EATING CRAB, YOU GET TWICE THE GOODNESS: ZINC AND PROTEIN-RICH CRABS AND OYSTERS!

NRG-Food

Does your mind wander if you have to listen to hours of dull and pointless presentations? Try these energy 'burgers', Full of protein, they'll help you stay attentive and on the bo so you can impress the board with that all-important question no one else thought of!

Adrenaline-Rush Crab Cakes

Thrill your dinner guests with this stunning fish dish. It's hot! It's spicy! It's sensational!

SERVES 4

WHAT TO BUY

+ 900 g/2 lb floury potatoes, peeled
+ Salt and pepper
+ 3 tbsp olive oil
+ 1 onion, finely chopped
+ 2 garlic cloves, crushed
+ 1 cm/½ in cube fresh ginger, very finely chopped
+ 2 tbsp Thai red curry paste
+ 175 g/6 oz can white crab meat, drained
+ 3 tbsp fresh coriander (cilantro), chopped
+ Flour for dusting
+ 3 tbsp vegetable oil

HOW TO COOK IT

1 Quarter the potatoes and cook them for about 15-20 minutes in a large pan of salted boiling water until just done. Drain and mash potatoes; season to taste.

2 Heat 1 tbsp of the oil in a frying pan and fry the onion, garlic, and ginger for about 5 minutes, or until soft but not browned. Stir into the mashed potato together with the curry paste, crab meat, and coriander (cilantro).

3 With floured hands, divide the mixture into 8 equal portions and shape into small patties.

4 Heat the remaining oil in a large frying pan and fry the crab cakes in batches for about 5 minutes on each side, until golden. Remove from the pan and pat dry on kitchen paper. Keep warm while cooking the remaining cakes. Serve with a hot sauce and let the credits roll.

Brain-Booster Swordfish & Bean Salsa

Give yourself that extra edge that you need to suceed in the corporate jungle. This protein-packed dish is top-grade brain fuel.

SERVES 4

WHAT TO BUY

+ 4 swordfish steaks
+ 2 tbsp vegetable oil

For the dressing:

+ 75 ml/2 ½ fl oz/⅓ cup olive oil
+ 4 tbsp fresh lime juice
+ I garlic clove, crushed
+ ½ tsp each ground cumin and coriander
+ Salt and pepper

For the salsa:

+ 450 g/I lb cooked black beans, drained
+ 450 g/I lb sweetcorn kernels
+ I red (bell) pepper, seeded and chopped
+ I yellow (bell) pepper, seeded and chopped
+ 2 small red chilies, seeded and finely chopped
+ I small onion, finely chopped
+ I large tomato, chopped
+ I large handful fresh coriander (cilantro) or parsley, finely chopped

How to cook it

1 Make the dressing: whisk the olive oil and lime juice together in a bowl. Add garlic and spices, whisk and season to taste.

2 Make the salsa: in a large bowl, combine the beans, sweetcorn, (bell) peppers, chilies, onion, and tomato. Pour the dressing over the salad, and toss to mix.

3 Season the swordfish steaks. Heat the oil in a large frying pan, add the fish and fry on both sides for 3-5 minutes, depending on thickness.

4 Stir the coriander (cilantro) or parsley into the salad, Serve with the fish and a glass of fruity red wine—and the world will be your oyster (or your swordfish)!

Brainy Swords

SWORDFISH IS HIGH IN OMEGA-3S, WHICH WILL HELP YOU BECOME A BRAINBOX. AS AN ADDITIONAL BONUS, IT WILL ALSO PROTECT YOU FROM HEART ATTACKS, STROKES, OBESITY, INSOMNIA, AND ARTHRITIS.

LOVE OF FAME IS THE LAST THING EVEN LEARNED MEN CAN BEAR TO BE PARTED FROM...
(TACITUS)

Quick-as-a-Flash Beef

This quick-cooked stir-fry is full of flavor— serve it to your dinner guests and your success will be no mere flash-in-the-pan!

SERVES 4

WHAT TO BUY

+ 1 ½ tbsp cornflour (cornstarch)
+ ¼ tsp Chinese Five-spice Powder
+ 2 tbsp vegetable oil
+ 3 tbsp soy sauce
+ 350 g/12 oz rump (round) steak, cut into thin strips
+ 1 cm/½ in cube fresh ginger, chopped
+ 1 garlic clove, finely chopped
+ 175 g/6 oz broccoli
+ 1 red (bell) pepper, cut into thin strips
+ 1 bunch spring onions (scallions), sliced diagonally
+ 4 tbsp sherry
+ 2 tsp sesame oil
+ 1 tbsp sesame oil

HOW TO COOK IT

1 In a bowl, combine the cornflour (cornstarch), 1 tbsp of the vegetable oil, Chinese Five-spice Powder, and soy sauce. Add the beef strips and turn to coat evenly. Leave to marinate for at least 30 minutes.

2 Heat the remaining oil in a wok or large frying pan. Remove the beef from the marinade, pat dry and stir-fry in the wok for 3–4 minutes, with the ginger and garlic.

3 Break the broccoli into florets, slice the stalk diagonally into thin ovals, and the florets into small heads.

4 Add the broccoli, (bell) pepper, and spring onions (scallions), and stir-fry for 2 minutes.

5 Combine the sherry with the sesame oil and 2tbsp water. Add the liquid to the wok and cover with a lid. Cook for 1 minute.

6 Transfer to warmed serving plates and serve immediately with rice or noodles, and a shot of sake. Write a timetable for your career progress.

Miracle Food

BROCCOLI IS A HIGH-OCTANE VEGETABLE, RICH IN VITAMINS A, B2, B6, AND C, AND THE MINERALS POTASSIUM, MAGNESIUM, AND ZINC. IT WILL GIVE YOU ENERGY, GOOD SKIN AND VISION, IMMUNITY, AND MAKE YOU GENERALLY INVINCIBLE. MAKE SURE YOU DON'T OVERCOOK THE BROCCOLI, AS THIS WOULD DIMINISH ITS POWER.

CHAPTER 2

Knock 'em out

IMPRESS YOUR DINERS WITH THESE DAZZLINGLY DESIRABLE DISHES

GLAMOROUS FOOD AND SPECTACULAR PRESENTATION —THEY'LL BE BOWLED OVER...

Contents

Show-Stealing Salmon Baguettes

Put yourself in the limelight with this show-stopping little number–your guests will really know you've arrived!

MAKES 20

WHAT TO BUY

+ 6 sheets of white gelatin
+ ½ lemon
+ 1 bunch fresh dill, chopped
+ 200 g/7 oz smoked salmon
+ 2 tbsp crème fraîche
+ 100 g/4oz whipping cream
+ Salt and pepper
+ ½ tsp paprika
+ 1 baguette, cut into 20 thin slices
+ 50 g/2 oz herb cream cheese
+ ½ cucumber, thinly sliced
+ Lemon wedges, to garnish

HOW TO COOK IT

1 Soak the gelatin in cold water, following instructions. Grate the zest of the lemon, squeeze out the juice.

2 Whizz the salmon together with the crème fraîche and the dill in the blender. Lightly squeeze out the gelatin, then dissolve it in a cup of hot water. Stir into the salmon purée, a bit at a time.

3 Whip the cream and fold into the salmon purée. Season to taste with salt, pepper, lemon zest, lemon juice and paprika. Cover and chill for 1 hour.

4 Meanwhile spread the baguette slices thinly with the cream cheese. Place a couple of cucumber slices on each one.

5 Stir the salmon mousse and fill into a piping bag with large star nozzle. Pipe onto the baguette slices and garnish with more dill and lemon wedges.

6 Crack open a bottle of Champagne and let the world know that you've arrived!

Crowning Glory Lamb

Roll out the red carpet! Cue the trumpets! This spectacular dish really will make you and your guests feel like royalty.

SERVES 6

WHAT TO BUY

+ 2 best ends of neck of lamb, each with 6 cutlets
+ 25 g/l oz butter
+ I onion, chopped
+ 3 celery sticks, chopped
+ I apple, peeled, cored, and chopped
+ 40 g/l ½ oz dried apricots, chopped
+ 125 g/4 ½ oz fresh breadcrumbs
+ 2 tbsp fresh parsley, chopped
+ Finely grated zest of ½ lemon
+ I tbsp lemon juice
+ I egg
+ Salt and pepper
+ 2 tbsp vegetable oil
+ I tbsp flour
+ 300 ml/10 fl oz lamb stock

HOW TO COOK IT

1 Trim each cutlet bone to a depth of 2.5 cm/ I in and trim off excess fat. Bend joints around, fat side inwards, and sew together using strong cotton or fine string to form a crown. Cover the exposed bones with foil.

2 Heat the oven to 180°C/350°F/Gas Mark 4. Melt the butter in a saucepan and cook the onion, celery, and apple until brown. Add the apricots, breadcrumbs, parsley, lemon zest and juice, and egg. Season to taste. Allow to cool. Fill the center of the joint with stuffing and weigh.

3 Calculate the cooking time: 25 minutes per 450 g/ 1 lb plus 25 minutes. Place the joint in a small roasting tin and baste it with the oil. Roast in the oven, basting occasionally. Cover with foil if necessary.

4 Transfer the crown roast to a warmed serving dish and keep warm. Skim off the fat in the roasting tin, add the flour and blend well with the roasting juices. Cook for 2–3 minutes, stirring continuously. Add the stock and boil for 2–3 minutes. Season and serve hot with the joint.

Guard of Honor.

THERE IS ANOTHER, EQUALLY SPECTACULAR DISH MADE FROM TWO BEST ENDS OF LAMB NECK: THE GUARD OF HONOR, WHICH INTERWEAVES THE BONES LIKE THE FINGERS OF TWO HANDS. MAKE THE EXPERIENCE COMPLETE BY SERVING IT WITH DUCHESS POTATOES, PRINCESS PEAS, AND A BOTTLE OF CHÂTEAU LATOUR BORDEAUX.

THIS WINE SHOULD BE EATEN, IT IS TOO GOOD TO BE DRUNK...
(JONATHAN SWIFT)

Flamin' Fillets of Pork

Put your name up in lights with these flame-cooked fillets. You'll be the toast of Broadway!

SERVES 4

WHAT TO BUY

+ 1 apple
+ 4 pork thinly cut fillets
+ Salt and pepper
+ 2 tbsp lemon juice
+ 50 g/2 oz butter
+ 4 tbsp Calvados
+ 300 ml/10 fl oz thick (heavy) cream

HOW TO COOK IT

1 Peel and core the apple, then cut into small dice.

2 Flatten the pork fillets between two sheets of clingfilm (plastic wrap), then season them generously with salt, pepper, and lemon juice.

3 Heat the butter in a large frying pan, and when it starts to foam, add the pork fillets. Fry over a high heat for about 5 minutes, so they change color, then reduce the heat and add the apple.

4 (Do the following step preferably with everyone watching for extra impact.) In a small saucepan, heat the Calvados. Take a ladle full, set light to it, and pour it flaming over the meat, while turning up the heat. Carefully add the remaining Calvados. Shake and move the pan so the flames spread, until they die down.

5 Reduce the heat and pour in the cream. Simmer gently for 2–3 minutes, stirring the sauce and scraping in the pan juices. When the cream has thickened, transfer the fillets to warm serving plates, top with the apple dice, and pour over the sauce.

6 Serve and delight in the rapturous applause.

THE ONLY REAL STUMBLING BLOCK IS FEAR OF FAILURE. IN COOKING (AND IN LIFE) YOU'VE GOT TO HAVE A WHAT-THE-HELL ATTITUDE...
(JULIA CHILD)

Practice Perfect

FLAMBÉING IS A SPECTACULAR WAY OF ADDING FLAVOR TO ANY FOOD, WHETHER SAVORY OR SWEET. A HIGH-ALCOHOL DRINK, SUCH AS BRANDY OR RUM, IS SET ALIGHT AND ADDED TO THE FOOD. THE FLAMES BURN OFF THE ALCOHOL, WHILE LEAVING THE FLAVOR. FOR MAXIMUM IMPACT—AND SAFETY—IT IS BEST TO PRACTICE FLAMBÉING ON YOUR OWN, WITHOUT GUESTS.

Dressed-to-Kill Sea Bass

Watch out-this fish means business. Serve with respect, and ask its permission first!

SERVES 4

WHAT TO BUY

+ 40 g/1 ½ oz couscous
+ 25 g/1 oz blanched almonds, finely chopped
+ 1 spring onion (scallion), thinly sliced
+ Salt and pepper
+ 1 large egg
+ 4 sea bass fillets, about 250g/8oz each, cleaned and scaled

For the salsa:

+ 4 tomatoes
+ 1 red onion, chopped
+ 1 small red chili, seeded and chopped
+ 2 tbsp fresh mint, chopped
+ 5 tbsp olive oil
+ Zest and juice of 1 lime

HOW TO COOK IT

1 Make the salsa: plunge the tomatoes into boiling water for 1 minute, then skin them. Halve, remove the seeds, and roughly chop the flesh. Combine with the onion, chili, and half the mint. Add 3tbsp oil and the lime zest and juice and stir well to combine.

2 In a bowl, combine the couscous, almonds, spring onion (scallion), and the remaining mint. Season.

3 Crack the egg on one plate and beat, then spread the couscous mixture on a second plate. Dip the sea bass fillets first in the egg, then in the couscous, making sure they are evenly coated all over.

4 Heat the remaining oil in a large frying pan. Add the fish and fry for about 5–10 minutes, turning once. Check that the fish is done: the flesh should flake easily when gently pulled with a fork,

5 Carefully transfer the fish to plates, making sure the couscous doesn't come off; serve with the salsa. Don't let the fish show you up–wear your best evening gear when serving this dish.

I LIKE A COOK WHO SMILES OUT LOUD WHEN HE TASTES HIS OWN WORK...
(R.F. CAPON)

Memory Boost

THIS ELEGANT FISH DISH IS A WINNER THANKS TO ITS UNUSUAL COATING. IT IS ALSO PACKED WITH MEMORY-ENHANCING MINERALS THAT HELP YOU RETAIN ANY BITS OF INFORMATION OR CASUAL REMARKS PASSED DURING DINNER–AND REMEMBER: KNOWLEDGE IS POWER!

Regal Chicken Supper

"I dub thee Sir Chicken." Well, maybe not, but you'll surely feel like a monarch when serving up this majestic meal.

SERVES 4

WHAT TO BUY

+ 2 tbsp olive oil
+ 4 chicken breasts, skinned and diced
+ 100 g/4 oz butter
+ 225 g/8 oz mushrooms, sliced
+ 1 green (bell) pepper, seeded and cut into strips
+ 2 tbsp plain (all-purpose) flour
+ 300 ml/10 fl oz chicken stock
+ 225 ml/8 fl oz/1 cup single (light) cream
+ 1 tbsp green peppercorns, drained
+ 1 bay leaf
+ A pinch of paprika
+ Salt and pepper
+ 2 egg yolks
+ 3 tbsp sherry
+ 1 small red chili, seeded and finely chopped

HOW TO COOK IT

1 Heat the oil in a large saucepan, add the chicken and brown for about 5 minutes, stirring occasionally. Remove and keep warm.

2 Melt the butter in the pan, add mushrooms and (bell) pepper and fry for about 5 minutes, or until softened. Add the flour, stir, and cook for 1–2 minutes. Slowly pour in the stock and the cream, stirring all the time. Bring to the boil, season with the peppercorns, bay leaf, paprika, and salt and pepper to taste. Cook for about 5 minutes.

3 Return the chicken to the pan. Put one ladle of the sauce into a small bowl and leave to cool a little. Stir in the egg yolks, then gradually pour back into the sauce. Do not boil again as the egg will curdle.

4 Add the sherry and the chili to the sauce, check the seasoning. Serve, or better still: do it in true royal style and have it served by your butler.

I'D LOVE TO LIVE AS A POOR MAN WITH LOTS OF MONEY...
(PICASSO)

Successful Bird

THE CHICKEN HAS CONQUERED THE WORLD, FROM RELATIVELY LATE BEGINNINGS. A DESCENDANT OF A MALAYSIAN BIRD, IT DID NOT REACH EUROPE UNTIL THE 5TH CENTURY, VIA PERSIA AND GREECE. TODAY IT IS HIGHLY PRIZED IN WESTERN COUNTRIES FOR ITS LEAN MEAT AND CULINARY VERSATILITY.

Fan-tastic Potatoes

***Open your own (potato) fan club with this
stunning recipe-your dinner guests will soon
be lining up to join!***

SERVES 4

WHAT TO BUY

+ 12 medium-sized baking potatoes (about 1.5 kg/
  3 ½ lb in total)
+ Salt and pepper
+ A drizzle of oil

For the herb filling:

+ 1 tbsp butter
+ 2 tbsp fresh parsley, chopped
+ 1 tbsp fresh oregano, chopped
+ 1 tbsp fresh basil, chopped
+ ½ tbsp fresh thyme, chopped

For the chili filling:

+ 1 tbsp olive oil
+ 1 tsp paprika
+ 1 small red chili, seeded and finely chopped
+ 1 tsp fresh coriander (cilantro), chopped

For the garlic filling:

+ 2 garlic cloves, finely chopped
+ ½ lemon
+ 1 tsp fresh rosemary, chopped
+ 1 tbsp olive oil

HOW TO COOK IT

1 Cut off a thin slice at the base of one of the flat sides
of each potato, so that they will lie on the baking tray

more easily. Cut each potato into thin slices, making sure you do not cut through, so that the slices will still be connected along the base. Place all the potatoes on a baking tray. Heat oven to 180°C/350°F/Gas Mark 4.

2 Melt the butter and stir in the herbs. Drizzle four of the potatoes with this mixture.

3 Stir the paprika into the oil and drizzle the mixture over four more potatoes. Sprinkle over the chili and the fresh coriander (cilantro).

4 Grate the zest of the lemon and squeeze out the juice. Combine the zest with the garlic and the rosemary. Drizzle the remaining potatoes with olive oil and lemon juice, then distribute the garlic mixture over them.

5 Bake the potatoes for about 1 hour, or until crisp and golden. Serve on their own as a stunning snack, or as a deeply impressive accompaniment with meat or fish.

MONEY IS THE ROOT OF ALL EVIL, AND YET IT IS SUCH A USEFUL ROOT THAT WE CANNOT GET ON WITHOUT IT ANY MORE THAN WE CAN WITHOUT POTATOES... (LOUISA MAY ALCOTT)

Perfect Pork with Plums

Serving up this rich, fruity casserole to your guests will give them a very clear message— you're on the fast track to success!

SERVES 4

WHAT TO BUY

- ✦ 2 tbsp groundnut oil
- ✦ 4 large pork chops, about 225 g/8 oz each
- ✦ Salt and pepper
- ✦ 2 tbsp light brown sugar
- ✦ 4 tbsp soy sauce
- ✦ 125 ml/4 fl oz/½ cup white wine
- ✦ 4 tbsp sherry
- ✦ 16 plums, halved and stoned
- ✦ A little fresh parsley, chopped

HOW TO COOK IT

1 Heat the oil in a casserole dish and fry the chops for a minute or so on each side until they have colored slightly. Season generously.

2 Add the sugar, soy sauce, wine, and sherry. Bring slowly to the boil, add the plums, and cover with a lid, then reduce the heat and leave to simmer very gently for 50 minutes, or until the chops are cooked: if prodded with a sharp knife, the meat should easily come away from the bone.

3 Lift out the chops, transfer to a warm plate, and keep warm. Turn up the heat under the sauce, and bring to the boil. Continue cooking for about 5 minutes, or until the sauce is reduced and looks glossy.

4 Using a fork, mash the plums into the sauce, then return the chops to the pan. Cook for another 2 minutes, or until the pork is warmed through.

5 Scatter with the chopped parsley, serve with boiled potatoes, and wait for all the questions to roll in: "where did you get this fantastic recipe?"

Money-Makers

THE GERMANIC TRIBES LIKED PORK LONG BEFORE THE ROMANS ARRIVED TO CONQUER THEIR RESPECTIVE COUNTRIES. THE WESTPHALIANS MADE LARGE AMOUNTS OF MONEY BY SELLING THEIR PRIZED SALTED AND SMOKED HAMS TO THE ROMAN INVADERS.

CONFIDENCE IS THE HINGE ON THE DOOR TO SUCCESS... (MARY O'HARE DUMAS)

Attractive Vegetable Gratin

This delectable dish is sure to have your popularity index rising. It's a mutually beneficial merger of cheese and vegetables. Just be sure you get your share!

SERVES 4

WHAT TO BUY

+ 1 large aubergine (eggplant), sliced
+ 1 onion, sliced
+ 1 tbsp olive oil
+ 3 tbsp breadcrumbs
+ 2 large courgettes (zucchini)
+ 2 tomatoes, sliced
+ 1 red (bell) pepper, seeded and cut into chunks
+ 1 yellow (bell) pepper, seeded and cut into chunks
+ Salt and pepper

For the gratin topping:

+ 5 slices white bread
+ 225 ml/8 fl oz/1 cup milk
+ 1 bunch flat-leaf parsley, finely chopped
+ 2 sprigs fresh marjoram, finely chopped
+ 3 garlic cloves, finely chopped
+ 150 g/5 oz Gorgonzola
+ Salt and pepper
+ 4 tbsp olive oil

HOW TO COOK IT

1 Cook the aubergine (eggplant) and onion slices in plenty of lightly salted boiling water for about 3 minutes. Drain in a sieve.

46

2 Heat the oven to 220°C/425°F/Gas Mark 7. Brush a large shallow baking dish with the olive oil, then sprinkle with the breadcrumbs. Pack all the vegetable slices and chunks into the dish, arranged almost vertically and closely together. Season to taste.

3 Cut the rinds off the white bread, place in a bowl and pour over the milk. Leave to soak for 5 minutes.

4 Mash the soaked bread with a fork, add the chopped herbs and garlic, crumble in the cheese, and mix well. Season to taste. Spread the bread-cheese-mixture evenly over the vegetables and drizzle with olive oil. Bake the gratin for about 30 minutes, or until golden brown and crusty on top.

5 Serve with a full-bodied Italian wine such as a Barbera or a Californian Cabernet Sauvignon.

> **THE SECRET OF SUCCESS IS TO KNOW SOMETHING NOBODY ELSE KNOWS...**
> **(ARISTOTLE ONASSIS)**

Starry Nights Cocktails Self-Starter

You'll shine like a star after drinking one of these coruscating cocktails. But don't have too many, or you may go into orbit!

MAKES 2

WHAT TO BUY

+ 4 parts gin
+ 2 parts Lillet Blanc
+ 1 part apricot brandy
+ A dash of Pernod
+ Plenty of crushed ice

HOW TO MAKE IT

1 Put all the ingredients into a shaker, fill up with plenty crushed ice and shake vigorously.

2 Strain the cocktail into chilled glasses and watch your career progress in leaps and bounds.

DRUNK IS FEELING SOPHISTICATED WHEN YOU CAN'T SAY IT... (ANON)

Star Cocktail

**Sip it and feel like you'll live forever.
Remember what that other star, Gloria
Swanson, once said: "A star is timeless!"**

MAKES 2

WHAT TO BUY

✦ 4 parts Calvados or apple brandy
✦ 2 parts sweet vermouth
✦ A dash of Angostura bitters
✦ A twist of lemon

HOW TO MAKE IT

1 Put all the ingredients except for the lemon into a
shaker together with crushed ice and shake vigorously.
2 Strain into chilled glasses, decorate with the twist of
lemon. Remember you're the star of the evening (and
make sure everyone else knows it!).

Celebration Cocktails
Diamond Fizz

Be a legend in your own living-room with this classic cocktail-serve it to your guests and your name will live forever.

SERVES 2

WHAT TO BUY

+ 4 parts gin
+ 1 part fresh lemon juice
+ 1 tsp sugar
+ Champagne or sparkling wine
+ Plenty of crushed ice
+ Ice cubes

HOW TO MAKE IT

1 Put all the ingredients except for the Champagne into a shaker together with crushed ice and shake vigorously.
2 Pour over ice cubes into chilled Champagne flutes, stir very gently and remember: diamonds are forever!

ONE MORE DRINK AND I'D BE UNDER THE HOST...
(DOROTHY PARKER)

50

Grand Occasion

You've found out you're related to Bill Gates, you've inherited a small Caribbean island, you've invented an antidote to stress— whatever the occasion, here's how to celebrate in grand style.

SERVES 2

WHAT TO BUY

+ 4 parts white rum
+ 1 part orange liqueur
+ 1 part white crème de cacao
+ 1 part fresh lemon juice
+ Ice cubes

HOW TO MAKE IT

1 Put all the ingredients into a shaker together with crushed ice and shake vigorously.

2 Strain into chilled glasses and prepare to give a celebratory speech to mark the grand event.

CHAPTER 3

Immortal Souls

SUPERSTAR SECRETS—ENJOY THE DISHES CREATED BY CELEBRITIES

LET THESE CELEBRITY DISHES INSPIRE YOU, AND BROADCAST YOUR NAME AROUND THE WORLD...

Contents

Chicken Tetrazzini Treat

Hit the highest notes with this delicious pasta favorite named after an Italian opera diva.

SERVES 4-6

+ 450 g/1 lb cooked chicken, diced
+ 225 g/8 oz Parmesan cheese, grated

WHAT TO BUY

+ 225 g/8 oz pasta shapes
+ 3 tbsp butter
+ 1 onion, chopped
+ 1 garlic clove, crushed
+ 2 tbsp flour
+ 475 ml/16 fl oz/2 cups chicken stock, hot
+ 125 ml/4 fl oz/½ cup milk
+ 2 tsp dry vermouth or sherry
+ 225 g/8 oz mushrooms, sliced
+ 1 tsp lemon juice
+ Salt and pepper

HOW TO COOK IT

1 Cook the pasta according to instructions until al dente.

2 Meanwhile, in a saucepan, melt the butter, add the onion and garlic, and cook for about 5 minutes until softened. Stir in the flour to make a smooth paste, add the chicken stock, stirring continuously. Pour in the milk and vermouth or sherry. Cook until thickened.

3 Stir in the mushrooms, lemon juice, salt, pepper, chicken, and drained pasta.

4 Stir in half the Parmesan cheese, sprinkle over the remainder and brown under the grill. Serve piping hot— the applause will be ringing in your ears.

Signor Caesar's Salad

You don't need a palace to rustle up this delicious salad-a classic from California's golden years.

SERVES 4

WHAT TO BUY

+ 2 slices white bread
+ 3 garlic cloves
+ 75 g/3 oz bacon, finely chopped
+ 3 tbsp vegetable oil
+ 2 small heads iceberg or Romano lettuce
+ 4 anchovy fillets
+ 50 g/2 oz Parmesan, shaved

For the dressing:

+ 2 eggs
+ 4 tbsp olive oil
+ 3 tbsp lemon juice
+ 1/2 tsp Worcestershire sauce
+ Salt and pepper

HOW TO COOK IT

1 Cut the crusts off the white bread, then cut the bread into 1 cm/1/2 in cubes. Peel and chop two of the garlic cloves and crush with a little salt, using a fork.

2 Heat a frying pan without adding any oil, then fry the bacon in it until crisp. Remove from the pan, add the oil to the pan and fry the bread cubes until they are golden, turning them once. Add the chopped garlic. Remove and pat dry on kitchen paper. Shred the lettuce leaves.

3 Make the dressing: cook the eggs for 1 minute in boiling water, then remove and crack into a bowl. Add

56

the oil, lemon juice and Worcestershire sauce to the eggs and stir until well mixed. Season to taste.

4 Peel and halve the third garlic clove. Rub the inside of a salad bowl with it. Put the lettuce, bacon, and anchovies into the bowl and combine with the dressing. Sprinkle the garlic croûtons and the Parmesan shavings over the top and serve—you'll feel like a Hollywood star!

IN THE FUTURE, EVERYONE WILL BE FAMOUS FOR 15 MINUTES... (ANDY WARHOL)

Wad of Lettuce

CAESAR CARDINI PROBABLY MADE MADE A WAD OF LETTUCE (THAT IS, A ROLL OF DOLLAR BILLS) WITH THIS FAB SALAD HE CREATED IN THE 1920S, IN HIS RESTAURANT NEAR THE MEXICAN BORDER. TODAY HIS NAME, LIKE HIS SALAD, IS ON EVERYONE'S TONGUE. IT'S THE ULTIMATE IN NAME-DROPPING: JUST CREATE YOUR OWN DISH AND NAME IT AFTER YOURSELF!

Best Beef Wellington

Conquer a hungry multitude with this meaty feast-a triumph of the culinary arts!

SERVES 8

WHAT TO BUY

+ 1.5 kg/3 ½ lb beef tenderloin
+ Pepper
+ 2 tbsp vegetable oil
+ 50 g/2 oz butter
+ 225 g/8 oz button mushrooms, sliced
+ 175 g/6 oz smooth liver pâté
+ 375 g/13 oz packet puff pastry, defrosted if frozen
+ 1 egg, beaten, to glaze

HOW TO COOK IT

1 Heat the oven to 220°C/425°F/Gas Mark 7. Trim and tie up the beef to retain its shape. Season with pepper. Heat the oil in a large frying pan, add the meat and fry briskly on all sides to brown. Press down with a spoon while frying to seal the surface well.

2 Place the meat in a roasting tin and cook in the oven for 20 minutes, then allow to cool. Remove the string.

3 In a saucepan, heat the butter and fry the mushrooms until they are softened; leave to cool, then blend with the pâté.

4 Roll out the pastry to a rectangle, about 33 x 27 cm/ 13 x 11 in and 6 mm/¼ in thick.

5 Spread the pâté mixture down the center of the pastry. Place the meat in the middle. Brush the edges of the pastry with egg. Fold the pastry edges over lengthwise and turn the parcel over so that the join is underneath. Fold the ends of the pastry under the meat and place on a baking sheet.

6 Decorate with leaf shapes cut from the pastry trimmings. Glaze with the beaten egg and bake in the oven for 50 minutes, covering with foil after 25 minutes.

7 Play marching tunes and brass-band favorites— then serve this glorious dish on the battlefield of culinary conquests.

Old Boots

THE DUKE OF WELLINGTON (1769-1852) WAS FAMED FOR HIS STATESMANSHIP AND HIS VICTORY OVER NAPOLEON AT WATERLOO. THIS GLORIOUS DISH, HOWEVER, WAS PROBABLY NOT CREATED TO CELEBRATE HIS CAMPAIGNS ON THE BATTLEFIELD, NOR BECAUSE HE WAS RENOWNED AS A GOURMET—THE JOINT, IT WAS THOUGHT, RESEMBLED HIS BROWN SHINY BOOTS (WHICH WERE, OF COURSE, ALSO NAMED AFTER HIM).

FAME AND TRANQUILITY CAN NEVER BE BEDFELLOWS... (MONTAIGNE)

Beef Stroganoff

You'll be a star—or even a Tsar—with this flavorsome Russian recipe. Just follow the steppes below!

SERVES 4-6

WHAT TO BUY

+ 2 tbsp olive oil
+ I large onion, sliced
+ 2 cloves of garlic, crushed
+ 125 g/4 ½ oz mushrooms, sliced
+ 700 g/I ½ lb rump (round) steak, cut into thin strips
+ I50 ml/5fl oz red wine
+ 200 ml/7 fl oz single (light) cream
+ I tsp French mustard
+ I beef stock cube
+ 3 tbsp fresh parsley, chopped
+ 2 tsp cornflour (cornstarch), blended in cold water
+ Salt and pepper
+ 2 slices bread
+ Oil for shallow-frying

HOW TO COOK IT

1 Heat the olive oil in a large pan and add the onion, garlic, mushrooms, and steak. Cook for 6-8 minutes, stirring occasionally.

2 Stir in the wine, cream, mustard, stock cube, half the parsley, blended cornflour (cornstarch), and season to taste. Bring to the boil and simmer gently for about 5 minutes, stirring occasionally until the sauce has thickened a little.

3 Meanwhile, heat I tbsp oil in a frying pan. Cut the crusts off the bread, dice the bread, and fry the bread cubes in the oil for 1–2 minutes on each side until they are golden and crisp. Remove and drain on kitchen paper.

4 Transfer the stroganoff to a warm serving dish. Arrange the croûtons on top and sprinkle with the remaining parsley.

5 Consider creating a new dish that could be named after you, making you truly immortal.

Versatile Dish

THIS DELICIOUS BEEF DISH WAS CREATED AT A COOKERY COMPETITION IN ST PETERSBURG IN RUSSIA IN THE 1890S AND NAMED AFTER COUNT STROGANOFF, A MEMBER OF ONE OF RUSSIA'S RICHEST NOBLE FAMILIES. TODAY, THE BASIC RECIPE OF COOKING MEAT IN A MUSHROOM AND SOUR CREAM SAUCE HAS BEEN ADAPTED FOR MANY OTHER RECIPES, THERE'S PORK STROGANOFF, CHICKEN STROGANOFF, SALMON STROGANOFF... SO WHY NOT INVENT YOUR OWN VERSION?

BEEF IS THE SOUL OF COOKING...
(MARIE ANTOINE CAREME)

> *A MAN'S DREAMS ARE AN INDEX TO HIS GREATNESS...*
> *(RANDALL R. McBRIDE, JR.)*

GOING BANANAS

This wickedly delicious dessert was create
to honor Dick Foster, who helped the Vice
Committee clean up the French Quarter o
New Orleans in the 1950s. Hire a jazz be
when you serve this dish, and have them
play favorite tunes to celebrate your fame

Bananas, Mister Foster

Amaze your guests with this most spectacular of desserts. It'll put your dinner party in a different class altogether.

SERVES 4

WHAT TO BUY

+ 6 tbsp butter
+ 4 tbsp brown sugar
+ 4 ripe bananas, peeled and sliced lengthwise
+ ½ tsp cinnamon
+ 100 ml/4 fl oz/½cup banana liqueur
+ 225 ml/8 fl oz/1 cup white rum
+ 4 large scoops vanilla ice cream

HOW TO COOK IT

1 Melt the butter in a large frying pan. Add the sugar and stir in, until the sugar has dissolved.

2 Add the bananas and fry gently over a low heat. Sprinkle with cinnamon.

3 Take the pan into the dining room and place it on a table-top cooker. Now pour the banana liqueur and rum over the bananas and set alight. Shake the pan to distribute the flames evenly. When the flames have died down, pour the bananas and sauce over the ice cream, and see your guests' faces light up with admiration.

Gallery of Fame

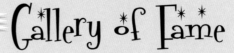

This swell dessert was created by one of the most famous chefs ever, the Frenchman Auguste Escoffier (although he denied it later). It was made in honor of one of the greatest opera singers, the Australian Dame Nellie Melba. Escoffier worked at the (equally famous) Ritz Hotel in London, and the Dame stunned her audiences at the (also famous) Covent Garden Opera House with her extraordinary coloratura soprano voice. The Dame was victorious in this battle for immortality—a toast was also named after her.

PEACH OF A TREE

Somewhere to the west of China, the Tree of Life is supposed to have grown, a peach tree belonging to the Royal Mother. It bore fruit only once in 3,000 years, and those who touched its sap would become luminous

Dame Melba's Peaches

Put a song in their hearts with this peaches-and-ice-cream dessert–a classic that will run forever.

SERVES 4

WHAT TO BUY

+ 400 g/14 oz fresh or frozen raspberries
+ 4 peaches
+ 125 ml/4 fl oz/½ cup whipping cream
+ 1 tbsp kirsch
+ 2 tbsp caster (superfine) sugar
+ 8 scoops of vanilla ice cream
+ ½ tbsp lemon juice

HOW TO COOK IT

1 Defrost the raspberries if frozen. Place them in a blender and whizz for a few seconds to a purée. Push the purée through a fine sieve to remove the seeds. Set aside.

2 Briefly plunge the peaches into boiling water, then slip off their skins. Halve the peaches, remove the stones, and slice the flesh. Whip the cream and flavor with the kirsch and 1 tbsp sugar.

3 Place two scoops of ice cream into the center of four dessert dishes. Arrange the peach slices around the ice cream. Sprinkle with the remaining sugar and drizzle with the lemon juice.

4 Spoon over the raspberry purée and serve with the whipped cream and a sensational rendition of your favorite aria (use the Dansette to go easy on your voice).

GET MY SWAN COSTUME READY... (PAVLOVA'S LAST WORDS)

Rags to Riches

Anna Pavlova's parents were poor, and she was a sickly child. Bu phenomenal talent propelled her to world fame, making her one the best known and wealthiest dancers of all times, the Dying S being her signature piece. Well there's hope for all of us then—w just need to tap into that hidden talent...

SWEET 'N' HEALTHY

Eggs are not as bad as their press: althou they're high in cholesterol, the body will adapt and make less of it. They do give y high-quality protein, iron for healthy blood and Vitamin D for healthy bones. All in al a dessert for go-getting winners.

Pretty Pavlova

Dance your way to success with this graceful dessert–truly la crème de la crème.

SERVES 4

WHAT TO BUY

+ 3 egg whites
+ A pinch of salt
+ 175 g/6 oz caster (superfine) sugar
+ 50 g/2 oz cup granulated sugar
+ 1 tbsp cornflour (cornstarch)
+ 1 tsp lemon juice
+ 300 ml/10 fl oz double (heavy) cream
+ 350 g/12 oz fresh raspberries

HOW TO COOK IT

1 Heat the oven to very low, about 130-140°C/250-270°F/Gas Mark ½-1. Beat the egg whites and salt until stiff peaks form. Gradually add the caster (superfine) sugar, beating all the time until it is all dissolved. By now it should be the consistency of thick cream. Mix the granulated sugar and cornflour (cornstarch) together and gently fold into the mix with the lemon juice.

2 Scoop the mixture in a perfect circle onto a baking tray and bake for 30-40 minutes. Allow to cool.

3 Whip the cream. Top the meringue circle with whipped cream and raspberries and serve–while performing a 'pas de deux'.

Tasty Tarte Tatin

The apples start at the bottom of this delicious pudding but rise gloriously to the top-just as you'll be doing very soon yourself!

MAKES 1 TART

WHAT TO BUY

+ 75 g/3 oz butter
+ 8 apples (about 1.3 kg/3 lb), peeled, cored and sliced
+ 100 g/4 oz sugar
+ 225 g/8 oz chilled butter
+ 700 g/1 ½ lb plain (all-purpose) flour
+ ½ tsp salt
+ 225 ml/8 fl oz/1 cup crème fraîche

HOW TO COOK IT

1 Melt the butter in a deep frying pan over a medium high heat. Stir in the apple slices and the sugar. Cook for about 20 minutes, stirring carefully so the apples and sugar do not stick. Increase the heat to high and cook for another 15 minutes, until the apples and sugar are golden brown and caramelized.

2 Make the pastry: cut the butter into thin slices, dice, or shavings. In a bowl, mix the flour, the butter pieces, and the salt together very lightly, so the butter is still visible. Add about 175 ml/6 fl oz/³/4 cup ice-cold water and mix very fast so it becomes a dough. Make sure the butter is still visible and not totally incorporated in the pastry. Wrap the pastry in clingfilm (plastic wrap) and chill for about 1 hour in the fridge.

3 Preheat the oven to 220°C/425°F/Gas Mark 7. Pile the apples into a round 25 cm/10 in baking dish. Roll out the pastry slightly larger than the baking dish, and place it on top of the apples, tucking the dough around the edges down into the dish.

4 Place the tart in the oven and bake for 35-40 minutes until golden brown. Serve with crème fraîche to pour over, and a glass of red wine or chilled cider for extra measures of success.

Lucky Error

THIS DISH OWES ITS EXISTENCE TO A MISTAKE. THE TATIN SISTERS RAN A HOTEL IN THE SOUTH-WEST OF FRANCE. ONE DAY, IN A RUSH, THEY FORGOT TO PUT THE PASTRY FOR THE APPLE PIE INTO THE TIN FIRST, AND THE APPLES HAD CARAMELIZED. SO THE INGENIOUS SISTERS JUST COOKED THEIR PIE UPSIDE-DOWN, WITH THE CRUST ON TOP, THEN TURNED IT OUT—TO RAPTUROUS APPLAUSE AND NEVER-ENDING SUCCESS!

> **SERVE THE DINNER BACKWARDS, DO ANYTHING—BUT FOR GOODNESS SAKE, DO SOMETHING WEIRD...
> (ELSA MAXWELL)**

Winning Sachertorte

Success will surely be within your grasp when you serve this deep, dark, satisfying chocolate cake from Vienna. It's a winner in any language!

MAKES 1 CAKE

WHAT TO BUY
+ 175 g/6 oz dark chocolate
+ 150 g/5 oz butter
+ 150 g/5 oz caster (superfine) sugar
+ 6 eggs, separated
+ 150 g/5 oz plain flour

For the icing and the filling:
+ 175 g/6 oz dark chocolate
+ 5 tbsp strong black coffee
+ 175 g/6 oz icing sugar
+ 6 tbsp apricot jam

+ 50g/2oz dark chocolate, for decorating the finished Sachertorte

HOW TO COOK IT
1 Heat the oven to 150°C/300°F/Gas Mark 2. Grease a 23 cm/9 in cake tin and line the base with baking paper. Melt the chocolate. In a bowl, beat the butter and half the sugar until pale and fluffy. Add the egg yolks and beat well. Add the chocolate, beating well. Sieve the flour into the mixture and fold it in. Whisk the egg whites until they stand in soft peaks. Add the remaining sugar to the egg whites and whisk in. Fold this into the chocolate mixture, half at a time.

2 Spoon the chocolate mixture into the prepared cake tin. Bake in the oven for about 1-1 ¼ hours. Remove and

cool for 5 minutes, then turn the cake onto a wire rack
to cool completely.

3 Make the icing: melt the chocolate in a bowl set over
a saucepan of boiling water. Beat in the coffee until
smooth. Sieve the icing sugar into a bowl, whisk in the
melted chocolate mixture to give a thick icing.

4 Halve the cake. Spread the jam over the bottom half
and sandwich the cake back together. Spread the icing
over the top and sides of the cake.

5 Pipe your name on the cake in melted chocolate.

Lucky Break

IN 1832, COUNT METTERNICH ASKED FOR A SPECIAL
DESSERT TO BE CREATED TO FLATTER HIS HONORED
GUESTS. THE TOP CHEF, HOWEVER, WAS ILL, AND THE TASK
FELL TO THE 16-YEAR-OLD APPRENTICE FRANZ SACHER.
HE WOULD BE PROUD: SOME 270,000 TORTES ARE
PRODUCED BY THE SACHER HOTEL EACH YEAR, AND THE
LARGEST ONE EVER MADE (2.5 M/8 FT) IS LISTED IN THE
GUINNESS BOOK OF RECORDS.

> **IS ELIZABETH
> TAYLOR FAT? HER
> FAVOURITE FOOD IS
> SECONDS...
> (JOAN RIVERS)**

Famously Drinkable Cocktails

Classic cocktails for some very classy folks!

Tom Collins

Time to celebrate your fame, make use of your wealth, and enjoy your good fortune...

WHAT TO BUY

+ Juice of 1 lemon
+ 1 tbsp caster (superfine) sugar
+ 4 parts gin
+ Soda water to top
+ 2 lemon slices
+ 2 cocktail cherries
+ Plenty of crushed ice
+ Ice cubes

HOW TO MAKE IT

1 Combine the lemon juice, sugar, and gin in a shaker with crushed ice, shake, then strain into tall glasses.
2 Add ice cubes and a good splash of soda water. Decorate the glass with a lemon slice and a cocktail cherry on a toothpick.

I DO NOT HAVE MORE THAN ONE DRINK BEFORE DINNER, BUT I DO LIKE THAT ONE TO BE LARGE AND VERY STRONG AND VERY COLD AND VERY WELL MADE... (JAMES BOND)

Harvey Wallbanger

This fabulously famous cocktail will give you all the clout you need to become ever more successful.

MAKES 2

WHAT TO BUY

+ 2 parts vodka
+ 8 parts orange juice
+ I part Galliano
+ Ice cubes

HOW TO MAKE IT

1 Pour the vodka and orange juice over ice cubes into two tall tumblers and stir well.

2 "Float" the Galliano: carefully pour it over the back of a teaspoon held close to the drink.

3 Serve without delay–and watch success story after success story just fall into your lap.

YOU'RE NOT DRUNK IF YOU CAN LIE ON THE FLOOR WITHOUT HOLDING ON... *(DEAN MARTIN)*

CHAPTER 4

Sweet Success

FINISH ON A HIGH NOTE WITH THESE
LUXURIOUSLY RICH DESSERTS

GO AHEAD—MAKE THEIR DAY, SERVE ONE OF THESE FANTASTIC DESSERTS TO ROUND OFF A PERFECT MEAL...

Contents

Successfully Smooth Zabaglione

Rich, smooth and altogether delightful-this delicious Italian dessert is surely a foretaste of how you will be in the very near future!

SERVES 4

WHAT TO BUY

+ 4 eggs, separated
+ 5 tbsp caster (superfine) sugar
+ 8 tbsp Marsala or sweet dessert wine
+ Almond macaroons, to serve

HOW TO COOK IT

1 Put the egg yolks into a bowl over a saucepan of simmering water. The bowl should not touch the water, and the water should simmer all the time.

2 Add the sugar and the Marsala or dessert wine to the egg yolks. Stir with a spoon to combine, then beat for about 15 minutes with a hand-held electric whisk until the mixture is thick, pale, and foamy.

3 When the zabaglione is cooked, carefully pour it into four tall glasses and serve immediately, with the almond macaroons. Enjoy each spoonful, and wait for appreciative "hmms" and "yums" to come from your guests and the 'family'.

Lord of the Castle

You know you were born for greatness. Serve up these opulent puddings to your guests and prove you can live like a lord!

SERVES 4

WHAT TO BUY

+ 100 g/4 oz butter
+ 100 g/4 oz caster (superfine) sugar
+ A few drops of vanilla essence
+ 2 eggs, beaten
+ 100 g/4 oz self-raising flour
+ 4 tbsp strawberry jam
+ 4 tbsp golden (corn) syrup
+ Custard, to serve

HOW TO COOK IT

1 Heat the oven to 180°C/350°F/Gas Mark 4. Grease 4 individual molds, and put an oiled sheet of baking paper into the bottom of each one.

2 In a bowl, cream together the butter and the sugar, beating them until pale and fluffy. Beat in the vanilla essence, and gradually add the beaten eggs, a little at a time. Add the flour, beat well to combine, until you have a smooth mixture.

3 Add 1 tbsp water and combine well. The mixture should now be so soft that it will easily slip off a spoon.

4 Place 1 tbsp of the strawberry jam into the bottom of each mold, then add the batter mixture, half-filling the molds and leaving enough room for the desserts to rise. Cover with a sheet of baking paper, place the molds on a baking tray and bake for about 25-30 minutes, or until firm and golden brown.

5 Remove molds from the oven and leave to cool for a few minutes. Remove the baking paper, and turn the "castles" out on to serving plates. Warm the syrup in a small saucepan and pour over the castles. Serve at the end of the banquet, with a goblet of your best mead.

> **FOOD, LIKE A LOVING TOUCH OR A GLIMPSE OF DIVINE POWER, HAS THE ABILITY TO COMFORT...**
> **(NORMAN KOLPAS)**

Easy Does It

SUGAR AND STARCH ARE MORE THAN JUST FIGURE-ENHANCING ESSENTIALS OF ANY DIET—THEY HELP CALM YOUR NERVES AND BRING ANY LATENT ANGER OR AGGRESSION UNDER CONTROL! SO, IF YOU FEEL THAT SUDDEN URGE TO RAM SOMEONE ELSE WITH YOUR CAR, OR TO SCREAM AT THE CHECK-OUT PERSON, JUST HAVE A CASTLE PUDDING INSTEAD—MUCH MORE CIVILIZED!

Champagne Granita Cup

Fizz your way to fame and fortune! Serve these sparkling cups to your guests, then shoot for the stars!

SERVES 4

WHAT TO BUY

+ 40 g/1 ½ oz caster (superfine) sugar
+ Juice of ½ lime
+ ½ bottle Champagne
+ A selection of tropical fruits (for example 1 pineapple ring, half a mango, half a papaya, and 2 kiwis, peeled, stones removed, and sliced)
+ 100 g/4 oz blackcurrants
+ 1 tbsp sugar
+ 1 tsp lemon juice

HOW TO COOK IT

1 In a bowl, combine the sugar and the lime juice. Stir in the Champagne, then pour the mixture into a shallow freezer-proof tray and freeze for about 2–3 hours. Remove from the freezer every half hour or so and, with a fork, break up the ice crystals that form around the edge of the dish. Stir the ice back into the center, and replace in the freezer.

2 Meanwhile make the blackcurrant sauce: remove the stalks from the blackcurrants. In a bowl, combine them with the sugar and the lemon juice and leave to rest for about 1 hour. Push the blackcurrants through a fine sieve to remove the seeds.

3 When the granita is ready, fill the fruits into chilled glasses. Scrape the granita out of the dish with a spoon and place on top of the fruits. Decorate the glasses with fresh fruit and pour over I tbsp sauce.

4 Sit back, enjoy, and wait for everyone to toast your good fortune with a glass of Champagne.

THE PROBLEM WITH SOME PEOPLE IS THAT, WHEN THEY AREN'T DRUNK, THEY'RE SOBER... (W.B. YEATS)

A Lot of Bottle

CHAMPAGNE, THE KING OF DRINKS, WILL MAKE YOU FEEL LIKE A CHAMPION, AND OTHERS WILL TREAT YOU AS SUCH, TOO. IT'S WORTH LEARNING SOME OF THE WINE WAITERS' TRICKS—FOR EXAMPLE, FOOLPROOF WAYS TO POP THE CORK, AND HOW TO POUR THE DRINK, HOLDING THE BOTTLE WITH ONE HAND ONLY. MUCH MORE IMPRESSIVE! IF THAT DOESN'T DO IT, SERVE A NEBUCHADNEZZAR—THE EQUIVALENT OF **20** BOTTLES! BET YOU WON'T HOLD THAT WITH ONE HAND!

Divine Divining Cookies

Leave nothing to chance! Become master of your own destiny with these oracular cookies. Write down your dreams, then make them come true!

MAKES ABOUT 20

WHAT TO BUY

+ 150 g/5 oz caster (superfine) sugar
+ 150 g/5 oz butter, softened
+ A few drops of vanilla essence
+ Grated zest of I lemon
+ I egg, beaten
+ 225 g/8 oz plain (all-purpose) flour

HOW TO COOK IT

1 Grease two baking sheets. With a fork or hand-held blender, cream together the sugar and the butter until frothy. Beat in the vanilla essence, lemon zest, and the beaten egg.

2 Blend in the flour and continue mixing until you have a firm paste. Knead, then cover with clingfilm (plastic wrap) and chill for 30 minutes.

3 Roll out the dough to a fat sausage shape, about 20 cm/8 in long and 5 cm/2 in diameter, wrap again in clingfilm (plastic wrap) and chill for 30 minutes.

4 Heat the oven to 190°C/375°F/Gas Mark 5. Cut the roll crossways into even slices, place them on a greased and floured baking tray and bake for about 15 minutes, or until golden brown.

5 Place the cookies on a wire rack to cool. Meanwhile prepare the fortune notes (see below). Once the cookies are cool, wrap each in in a fortune note and then in colorful foil. Serve in a large shallow bowl—and find out what the future holds in store.

Fortune Cookies

DAVID JUNG, WHO FOUNDED THE HONG KONG NOODLE COMPANY IN LOS ANGELES, IS CREDITED WITH HAVING INVENTED THE FORTUNE COOKIE IN 1918. SUPPOSEDLY, THE COOKIES WERE MEANT AS A SWEET TREAT FOR THE UNEMPLOYED MEN WHO GATHERED DAILY OUTSIDE HIS COMPANY, BUT PERHAPS HE WAS JUST AN EXCELLENT MARKETING MAN.

THIS RECIPE GIVES YOU THE OPPORTUNITY TO MAKE YOUR OWN. WRITE YOUR MESSAGES AND WRAP THE COOKIES IN THEM. THEY COULD, FOR EXAMPLE, PROMISE THE READER THAT "M WILL PROPOSE MARRIAGE", OR THAT "FAME LIVES AT NUMBER 23", OR THAT "MONEY WILL FOLLOW THE TUNE OF THE JAZZ BAND". JUST LET YOUR IMAGINATION RUN RIOT!

> *A BALANCED DIET IS A COOKIE IN EACH HAND...*
> *(ANON)*

Stylish Vodka Jellies

Get the sweet flavor of success with these zesty jellies-your dinner guests will be flushed with their good fortune too!

SERVES 4-6

WHAT TO BUY

+ 2-3 small sprigs fresh rosemary
+ 25 g/1 oz powdered gelatin
+ 100 g/4 oz caster (superfine) sugar
+ 600 ml/20 fl oz fresh orange juice
+ Zest of 1 lime
+ 150 ml/5 fl oz vodka

HOW TO COOK IT

1 Place the rosemary sprigs into a small saucepan, add 150 ml/5 fl oz water and bring to the boil. Turn off the heat and leave to infuse for at least 15 minutes.

2 Remove the rosemary sprigs and sprinkle the gelatin into the rosemary water. Leave for about 10 minutes, then heat over a gentle flame, stirring constantly, until the gelatin has dissolved.

3 Meanwhile, cut the lime zest into very fine strips. In a second saucepan, heat the zest together with the orange juice, the vodka, and the sugar. Stir until the sugar has completely dissolved. Remove the zest with a slotted spoon and reserve.

4 Take both liquids off the heat and combine, whisking vigorously to blend together. Leave to cool a little, then

84

pour the jelly mixture into cocktail glasses. Leave to set, then garnish the glasses with the reserved lime zest and phone the Kremlin–they will want to be informed.

EVEN MONKS IMBIBE... (ANTON CHEKHOV)

Water of Life

VODKA WAS CONSIDERED A FANTASTIC HEALTH–GIVING DRINK. IN THE 12TH CENTURY, THE FAMOUS SCHOOL OF MEDICINE AT SALERNO IN ITALY USED LARGE AMOUNTS OF THIS MIRACULOUS MEDICATION TO CURE ALL KINDS OF AILMENTS. A HUNDRED YEARS LATER, THE ALCHEMIST ARNAUD DE VILLENEUVE WAS STILL CONVINCED THAT VODKA WOULD 'STRENGTHEN THE BODY AND LENGTHEN THE LIFE'. TODAY IT IS STILL KNOWN AS ONE OF THE PUREST SPIRITS AROUND, AND SOME PEOPLE CLAIM THAT YOU CAN'T GET A HANGOVER FROM IT, HOWEVER MUCH YOU DRINK! WORTH CHECKING OUT?

> *WHAT YOU SEE BEFORE YOU, MY FRIEND, IS THE RESULT OF A LIFETIME OF CHOCOLATE...*
> *(KATHERINE HEPBURN)*

Chocolate Happiness

CHOCOLATE CONTAINS LOADS OF THEOBROMINE—A SUBSTANCE SIMILAR TO THE HORMONES PRODUCED BY THE BRAINS OF PEOPLE WHO HAVE FALLEN I LOVE. IT MAKES YOU FEEL GOOD, AND IF YOU ARE HAPPY WITH YOURSELF YOU PROJECT A CONFIDENT SELF-IMAGE, AND SUCCESS WILL FOLLOW.

FINGER-LICKIN' GOOD

The secret of this sweet treat lies in the f that each little box presents a multitude o sins—ice cream, chocolate, fruit. Make sure you get the exclusive rights on the recipe, and reap the rewards.

Hold-The-Front-Page Treats

These little boxes of delight really are headline news! Serve them at your dinner party, and watch as your guests 'scoop' them into their mouths!

What to Buy

+ 475 ml/16 fl oz block chocolate ice cream
+ 24 peppermint chocolate wafers
+ 150 ml/5 fl oz whipping cream
+ 300 g/11 oz can mandarins or maraschino cherries, drained
+ 6 small mint sprigs

How to Cook It

1 Cut the ice cream into six even-sized cubes. Press the chocolate wafers onto the four sides of each cube, leaving the tops and bottoms plain. Be careful not to break the wafers as you press them on. Return the ice cream boxes to the freezer.

2 When you are ready to serve the cubes, whip the cream until thick. Fill it into a piping bag, and pipe a whipped cream swirl on top of each box. Decorate with mandarins or cherries and mint sprigs.

3 Serve immediately on chilled plates. Wait for the admiring "wows!" from your invitees—they'll have never seen or eaten anything like it!—and beam the news around the world.

SINGLENESS OF PURPOSE IS ONE OF THE CHIEF ESSENTIALS FOR SUCCESS IN LIFE, NO MATTER WHAT MAY BE ONE'S AIM...
(JOHN D. ROCKEFELLER)

LIQUID GOLD

When Cortez, the Spanish conquistador, met the emperor Montezuma and asked where he might keep his gold, he was led to a cocoa tree. After a fortnight of festivities, the Spanish were finally served some frothing chocolate—in 2,000 fine gold cups!

Rockefeller Fridge Cake

Make sure you have one of these rich chocolate cakes in your fridge. It's good to keep a cool head when you decide how to spend your next million.

SERVES 6

WHAT TO BUY

+ 20 shortbread biscuits (cookies)
+ 175 g/6 oz butter, softened
+ 175 g/6 oz caster (superfine) sugar
+ 2 egg yolks
+ 125 g/5 oz dark chocolate
+ 1 tbsp brandy or kirsch

HOW TO COOK IT

1 Grease a 450 g/1 lb loaf tin. Line the base and sides with baking paper, then line the base with the biscuits (cookies), trimming them to fit if necessary.

2 In a bowl, cream together the butter and the sugar, then beat in the egg yolks. Blend thoroughly.

3 Melt the chocolate in a bowl set over a pan of simmering water, let cool slightly but not set. Stir in the brandy or kirsch.

4 Spoon one-third of the choc mix into the tin, then cover with a layer of biscuits. Repeat layers, finishing with the chocolate. Chill until needed.

5 Serve with a cup of extra-strong coffee, and watch your shares climb relentlessly.

Magnificent Manor Muffins

Serve these most English of muffins and your guests really will believe you're 'to the manor born'.

SERVES 12

WHAT TO BUY

- ✦ 350 g/12 oz short-crust (unsweetened) pastry
- ✦ 6 egg yolks
- ✦ 100 g/4 oz soft brown sugar
- ✦ 425 ml/14 fl oz milk
- ✦ 200 ml/7 fl oz double (heavy) cream
- ✦ 1 vanilla pod, split
- ✦ 50 g/2 oz self-raising flour
- ✦ 25 g/1 oz butter
- ✦ 25 g/1 oz chopped almonds
- ✦ 225 g/8 oz raspberry jam

HOW TO COOK IT

1 Heat the oven to 200°C/400°F/Gas Mark 6. For the base, roll out the pastry to about 6mm/1/4 in thick. Cut out 12 circles with a 10 cm/4 in round cutter, and use to line a 12-hole muffin tin.

2 Press the pastry carefully into each hole, pinching the edges slightly so that they are a little higher than the tin. Prick the bases with a fork. Line each one with baking paper and a few baking beans or rice to weight the paper down. Chill for 1 hour.

3 Make the filling: in a bowl, combine egg yolks and 75 g/ 3 oz of the sugar. In a saucepan, heat the milk, cream, and vanilla over a gentle heat. Bring to just below boiling point. Add the milk to the egg mixture in the bowl, stirring constantly. Return both to a clean pan over a low heat. Continue stirring until it begins to thicken and coats the back of a spoon that is dipped into the mixture. Transfer to a bowl and cool, then chill over night.

4 Heat the oven to 200°C/400°F/Gas Mark 6. Rub together the remaining sugar, flour, butter, and almonds to make a crumble mix, then spread out on a baking tray. Remove the muffin tin from the fridge and place both the muffin tin and the crumble mix in the oven for 10 minutes, or until golden brown. Remove the paper and the beans from the pastry cases about 5 minutes before the cooking time is complete. Once golden, remove both tins from the oven, and allow to cool.

5 To assemble, take the pastry shells out of the tin and place a teaspoon of jam in the base of each one. Top with a teaspoon of custard and finish with a generous scattering of toasted crumble mix.

6 Ring the bell and ask all your guests to assemble in the afternoon room. Serve the muffins, with a cup of deliciously English tea.

I RECOLLECTED THE THOUGHTLESS SAYING OF A GREAT PRINCESS, WHO, ON BEING INFORMED THAT THE COUNTRY PEOPLE HAD NO BREAD, REPLIED, 'THEN LET THEM EAT CAKES!' (J.J. ROUSSEAU)

Magic Marzipans

Give fame and fortune a helping hand with these sophisticated marzipan fancies-they're guaranteed to work like a charm!

MAKES 24

WHAT TO BUY

+ 450 g/l lb marzipan
+ 25 g/l oz glacé cherries, chopped very finely
+ 25 g/l oz stem (preserved) ginger, chopped very finely
+ 50 g/2 oz dried apricots, chopped very finely
+ 350 g/12 oz dark chocolate
+ 25 g/l oz white chocolate
+ Icing (confectioner's) sugar, to dust

HOW TO COOK IT

1 Line a baking tray with baking paper. Divide the marzipan into three equal-sized balls and knead each in your hands one by one until soft.

2 Work the chopped glacé cherries into one marzipan portion by kneading both together on a surface that is lightly dusted with icing (confectioner's) sugar.

3 Work the chopped stem (preserved) ginger into the second ball of marzipan, and the dried apricots into the third ball, to flavor each portion individually.

4 Form each flavored portion into smaller balls, keeping the flavors separate.

5 Melt the dark chocolate in a bowl set over a saucepan of gently simmering water. Using a cocktail stick, pick up each ball and dip it into the chocolate to coat. Now place the balls in groups of the three flavors on the prepared baking sheet. Chill until set.

6 Melt the white chocolate in a bowl set over a saucepan of simmering water, and drizzle a little over the top of each group of marzipan balls. Chill again, to harden. Dust with icing (confectioner's) sugar, and wait for your lucky charms to work.

MONEY IS BETTER THAN POVERTY, IF ONLY FOR FINANCIAL REASONS... (WOODY ALLEN)

Pigs & Potatoes

MARZIPAN IS CONSIDERED A LUCKY CHARM IN MANY EUROPEAN COUNTRIES. IN SPAIN AND PORTUGAL, MARZIPAN FRUITS ARE POPULAR GIFTS, AND IN GERMANY MARZIPAN PIGS AND MARZIPAN POTATOES—MUCH LIKE THE SWEET SPHERES IN THIS RECIPE—ARE GIVEN AS LUCKY CHARMS FOR CHRISTMAS AND THE NEW YEAR.

Prize-Winning Pear Tart

The accolades will be coming thick and fast when you present this fabulous confection to your adoring dinner guests. Immortality beckons!

SERVES 6

WHAT TO BUY

+ I packet short-crust (unsweetened) pastry
+ 3 small pears
+ 250 g/9 oz full-fat soft cheese
+ 2 eggs
+ 3 tbsp icing (confectioner's) sugar
+ I tbsp lemon juice
+ I tsp almond essence
+ 25 g/I oz flaked almonds
+ Extra icing (confectioner's) sugar, to decorate

HOW TO COOK IT

1 Heat the oven to 200°C/400°F/Gas Mark 6. Roll out the pastry and press it into a 20 cm/8 in shallow-sided cake case. Place a sheet of baking paper on top and cover with baking beans or rice. Bake for 10 minutes. Remove the tart from the oven, set aside to cool a little, and reduce the oven temperature to 180°C/350°F/Gas Mark 4.

2 Meanwhile, halve the pears, peel three of the pear halves and remove all the cores. Cut each pear crossways into slices and lay the slices in the pastry case, alternating the peeled and the unpeeled pear halves, fanning out, so a pretty pattern emerges.

3 In a large bowl, beat together the soft cheese, eggs, icing (confectioner's) sugar, lemon juice, and almond essence until well mixed. Pour the mixture over the pears in the cake tin.

4 Sprinkle with the flaked almonds and return to the oven for about 1 hour, or until set and slightly golden.

5 Dredge the tart with icing (confectioner's) sugar, serve, and polish your acceptance speech.

'STRESSED' SPELLED BACKWARDS IS 'DESSERTS'. COINCIDENCE? I THINK NOT... (ANON)

Eaters Digest

ALMONDS ARE A HEALTHY SOURCE OF PROTEIN. PROTEIN CONTAINS AMINO-ACIDS WHICH THE BODY TURNS INTO NEUROTRANSMITTERS, CHEMICALS THAT PASS INFORMATION FROM ONE BRAIN CELL TO ANOTHER. PEARS ARE RICH IN DIETARY FIBER AND VITAMIN C. THIS TASTY TART THUS GIVES YOU A CLEAR, SHARP-THINKING MIND AND ALL-ROUND GOOD HEALTH, AS WELL AS A POSITIVE OUTLOOK. JUST WHAT YOU NEED TO BECOME RICH AND FAMOUS.

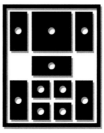